Unshakable

By

Rosze Kaur

About the Author

Rosze Kaur is an anointed teacher of God's Word. She was born and raised in Punjab, India in a small village called Awana. In 2001, she came to the United States of America in search of a better life. God has transformed the life of Rosze Kaur from Sikhism to Christianity. Rosze has dedicated her life to serving God and humanity. With unwavering compassion and faithfulness, it is her desire to help build hope into God's people that will help them to live a life of victory! Rosze Kaur's passion is to see other people win in life.

Contents

INTRODUCTION

Oxford Dictionary defines unshakeable as "something that cannot be shaken; but the Free dictionary defines unshakeable as marked by a firm determination or resolution; firm conviction; steadfast resolve or a man of unbending perseverance."

No matter what happens, you need to reach down into the deep roots of conviction and declare that "I will not bow down to the god of this world." Let it draw you closer to God, let it cause you to fall more deeply in love with Him.

God wants us to choose to love Him freely, even when the choice might cause us pain, because of our love for Him and through our knowledge of His great love for us.

Just because you can't see Jesus in the difficult circumstances, doesn't mean He is not there. Just because you can't hear Jesus doesn't mean He is not speaking. Have the faith to say "I'm trusting in what you are up to."

"I don't know what you are up to God, but I know you have a bigger plan" I believe this is a prophetic word for you today. I believe this is a prophetic word for this generation. God's got bigger plans for us. God has got bigger plans for this generation and individual. He has big plans! No matter what you are seeing, God's not finished. He will not fail you He knows what He is doing and He is in charge. Will you have an unbending faith in this mighty God and choose not to be **shaken**?

If you can understand God's unchangeable love it will help you put down deep roots in difficult times. His perfect, unshakeable, powerful, transcending, transforming love that goes beyond our human failures. That's His love patient, unsearchable, kind, never hurts us.

Things happen and you don't know why but God's got something better in store for you. If we can understand God's incredible love for us, it would stop us running away and cause us to run to Him.

If we put our roots down into His love, it matters not what situation we are in, He is able to deliver us from it; take us up to a new level. No matter what the circumstances, if you understand His love it will cause you to say; "I trust you God", and I know you will be able to have unshakeable faith to see Him bring His goodness, His deliverance and His plans and purposes for you.

To say He is the Lord, and my Savior, and I will submit all my ways unto Him.

Romans 8:31 "What, then, shall we say in response to these things? If God is for us, who can be against us?"

If God is for us, who can be against us? Simple and yet profound. God is for you. So, the question is, who or what is against us? And yet Paul is still able to say:

Romans 8:37 "No, in all these things we are more than conquerors through him who loved us."

Romans 8:38-39 *For I am convinced [and continue to be convinced beyond any doubt] that neither death, nor life, nor angels, nor principalities, nor things present and threatening, nor things to come, nor powers, nor height, nor depth, nor any other created thing, will be able to separate us from the [unlimited] love of God, which is in Christ Jesus our Lord."*

Daniel 3:4-6 & 16-18

Here are three young men with unshakeable faith, a conviction deep rooted in their revelation of who God is. Facing a fiery furnace, they tell the king that they do not need to defend themselves on this matter. Even more, they are able to say:

16 Shadrach, Meshach, and Abednego answered the king, "O Nebuchadnezzar, we do not need to answer you on this point.

17 If it be so, our God whom we serve is able to rescue us from the furnace of blazing fire, and He will rescue us from your hand, O king.

18 But even if He does not, let it be known to you, O king, that we are not going to serve your gods or worship the golden image that you have set up!"

Deep rooted, unshakeable faith that's what God says will come to pass, but even if it doesn't, we will not bow.

Being Unshakeable is based on conviction, not favorable circumstances.

1 Thess 1:5 "because our gospel came to you not only in word, but also in power and in the Holy Spirit and with full conviction. You know what kind of men we proved to be among you for your sake."

Conviction of God's infallible word. That the way to God is through conviction of sin and repentance. Our rock. These Hebrew boys were so strong in their convictions, they were prepared to die for them. They were captured at only 16 or 17 years of age but they were absolutely unshakable. This book is set to place you and enlighten you to stand firm and remain unshakable.

Be Unshakeable

"Wherefore I will not be negligent to put you always in remembrance of these things, though ye know them, and be established in the present truth. Yes, I think it meet, as long as I am in this tabernacle, to stir you up by putting you in remembrance. Knowing that shortly I must put off this my tabernacle, even as the Lord Jesus Christ hath shewed me. Moreover, I will endeavor that ye may be able after my decease to have these things always in remembrance" 2 Peter 1: 12-15 (KJV).

As believers, we sometimes tend to be complacent, forgetful, and uncommitted despite knowledge of the truth.

Out of Peter's awareness and concern, he pleaded with the believers to be steadfast in their walk with God and to hold fervently to the truth. He recognized that although they were established in the truth, being reminded constantly was essential. He did not want them to take the death, burial, and resurrection of our Lord for granted but be enthused and devoted as they live for God. Brethren, let us examine our attitudes when we are asked and encouraged to lay aside the baggage of this world and hold firmly to the hands of our savior.

We face similar challenges as the Christians of Peter's time, which is, having a roller coaster experience of being on the mountain top followed by being in the valley. It seems to stem from our forgetfulness of who He is and who we are in Him. Many of us can recall divine encounters where we are compelled to make commitments to change, yet we tend to fall short of our commitments. Peter's appeal is relevant to us as we fight the good fight of faith. May God help us to remember where He has brought us from.

God's Promises are True

"Whereby are given unto us exceeding great and precious promises." 2 Peter 1:4 (KJV)

"For I know the thoughts that I think toward you, saith the Lord, thoughts of peace, and not evil, to give you an expected end." Jeremiah 29:11 (KJV)

The promised blessing of salvation is very precious. It was first given in Genesis 3:15, with the promise that the seed of the woman (the promised Messiah.) would bruise the head of the enemy. This promise was fulfilled in the New Testament as recorded in Galatians 4:4-5, "But when the fulness of the time was come, God sent forth his Son, made of a woman, made under the law, to redeem them that were under the law, that we might receive the adoption of sons."

The great promise of the Holy Ghost in the New Testament (Luke24:49) was fulfilled on The Day of Pentecost, (Act 2:1-4). In addition, there are numerous other promises that God has given to us. A few of them are:

- If we search for Him we will find Him (Deuteronomy 4:29)
- Protection for His children (Psalm 121),
- He promised His love will never fail (1 Chronicles 16:34)
- Salvation to all who believe in His Son (Romans 1:16-17)
- He promised all things will work out for good for His children (Romans 8:28)
- Comfort in our trials (2 Corinthians 1, 3-4),

- A new life in Christ (2 Corinthians 5:17)
- He promised to finish the work He started in us (Philippians 1:6)

As humans we make and break promises daily, but what privilege we have knowing that God will not break His promises. God's promises are yea and amen. He does not take short cuts, gets fatigued or annoyed when fulfilling His promises. It is His delight and good pleasure to fulfill the promises of His words in our lives. We may feel undeserving or unworthy but we are not merited based on our own righteousness. It is the righteousness of Jesus that deems us worthy. He requires us to extend our faith to believe His words. "Abraham believed God, and it was counted unto him for righteousness." (Romans 4:3). At his age, with a barren wife the promise of a son seemed unreal, much more being the father of many nations; however, he believed God not knowing the pathway for it to be fulfilled.

Let us trust God with the outcome of every situation in our lives. Furthermore, His promises give us hope beyond this life. Where would we be without His promises? They may not be instant, so while we wait, we will pray and thank Him for His promises

Apply Patience

"And to knowledge temperance; and to temperance
patience" 2 Peter 1: 6.

Although life is good it has its share of speed bumps,
roadblocks and uncertainties. Whatever it is that pushes the
pause button on your life can sometimes seem intolerable,
especially for a lifestyle that is constantly on fast forward.

There is little room for patience. What then is patience? Why
is patience a requirement? The usage of the word 'patience'
in Latin is associated with calmness and composure.

1 Patience is to have the capacity to accept or tolerate delay
or problems without becoming annoyed or anxious.

2 We are encouraged to be patient during tribulation.
(Romans 12:12 KJV) A negative emotion almost always
follows delays, problems or sufferings.

While you have liberty to become angry when things go
wrong, is it an acceptable practice to allow resentment to
consume you? Ephesians 4:26 (KJV) Ever wonder why God
placed our souls in the unpredictable hands of our patience?
Luke says, "In your patience possess ye your souls" (Luke
21:19 KJV)

Has your patience been tested lately? Are you promised
something that you think God has forgotten? Be hopeful. Be
prayerful. God will not forget His promises. He said, "…I
will not forget you! See, I have written your name on the
palms of my hands…" (Isaiah 49:15-16 NLT). David was
promised the throne of Israel years prior to his crowning.

During the waiting period he suffered countless mishaps, especially at the hand of his predecessor, Saul, yet he remained patient and wise. (1 Samuel 18:7-12; 23:8; 24:1-15 KJV) Everything God has promised you will come to pass at the right time.

The Bible is filled with moral boosting assurances to lead you through life's challenges and help you accelerate to a higher level of patience.

Here are a few.

- "Let us not become weary in doing good, for at the proper time we will reap a harvest if we do not give up". (Galatians 6:9 NLT)
- "And we know that all things work together for good to them that love God..." (Romans 8:28 KJV)
- "But they who wait for the Lord shall renew their strength; they shall mount up with wings like eagles; they shall run and not be weary; they shall walk and not faint. (Isaiah 40:31 NLT)
- "For I know the plans I have for you, declares the Lord, plans for welfare and not for evil, to give you a future and a hope. (Jeremiah 29:11 NLT)

3 Maintain calmness and composure in all things as you add to your faith.

Held on to the Prophetic Word of God

"We have also a more sure word of prophecy" 2 Peter 1:19 (KJV)

Our salvation is grounded in the truth and reality of the gospel. It is definitely not a fable as presupposed by many. It is a prophetic declaration of the power of His coming, the Godhead and incarnation of our savior, which we have in the Old Testament. The Lord Jesus is the wonderful counsel of the holy and gracious God. It was foretold by the OT prophets who spoke and wrote as influenced and directed by the Holy Spirit. Therefore, Peter was determined to prove the veracity and reality of the gospel.

It should be noted that the description given in the Old Testament Scriptures is called "a more sure word of prophecy. The New Testament (NT) is a fulfillment of the Old Testament prophecies. The Old Testament is a more sure word of prophecy. It is to the Jews who received it as the oracles of God. Followed by prophets who confirmed what was delivered by those who went before, and these prophecies had been written by the express command, preserved with special care, and many of them fulfilled by the wonderful providence of God. Therefore, it was more certain to those who all along received and read the Scriptures than the Apostles' account of this voice from heaven. Moses and the prophets were persuaded more powerfully than the miracles observed or experienced.

Our faith should be firm because we have a sure word of prophecy. All the prophecies of the OT are more and certain to us who have the history of the most exact accomplishment

11

of them. The Apostle encouraged us to search the Scriptures. Further, he informed us that we do well if we take heed to them, that is, apply our minds to understand the sense, and hearts believe in the truth of this sure word; and to be bended, molded, and fashioned by it.

Take Heed

"Whereunto ye do well that ye take heed, as unto a light that shineth in a dark place until the day dawn, and the day star arise in your hearts" 2 Peter 1:19 (KJV).

Peter, in comparing the Old Testament prophecies and the apostles' testimony of the voice at the Transfiguration, is elevating the Word of God above all else. He is emphasizing here a more solid basis for faith than that of signs and wonders. He had seen our Lord Jesus Christ receive glory in the holy mountain and had seen visions and heard voices from Heaven. Nevertheless, he says we have something surer the Word of God.

The written word of God is certain and should be relied upon with more confidence than anything else. The apostle Paul reinforced this point when he said, *"But even if we or an angel from heaven should preach to you a gospel other than what we have preached to you, a curse be on him!"* (Galatians 1: 8 HCSB). Similarly, the sanctifying work of the Holy Spirit in our hearts and lives is a more certain and unquestionable evidence of our salvation than if an angel should come from heaven and testify to us. The Word of God is the revelation of God's will to us, and it, being the final authority, is the "sure word" that we are to give earnest heed and attend to: We have a more sure word of prophecy; whereunto ye do well that ye take heed (II Peter 19).

When someone lays a foundation, he or she then proceeds to build upon it, and so must we do. It is not sufficient merely to know that the Word of God is sure, we must proceed now to place our trust in it and govern our lives accordingly. We must not imagine that because we know of the truths contained in Scripture and are acquainted with the purposes for which they have been given, much benefit will be received from that alone. We must lay hold upon these truths, and feed on them daily. We must search and study them with careful diligence and attention, subject our consciences to the power of them, and order our conversations according to them. In this way our faith, instead of being shaken by the objections of the enemies of the gospel, may be more fully confirmed.

As we continue our journey, may we endeavor, like the prophet Jeremiah, to "esteem the words of His mouth more than my necessary food" (Jeremiah 23:12). Christ, then will have the preeminence in our lives and we will "attain to the unity of the faith and of the knowledge of the Son of God-a mature person, attaining to the measure of Christ's full stature." (Ephesians 4:13 NET)

Foundation of our Hope

"For we are saved by hope: but hope that is seen is not hope: for what a man seeth, why doth he yet hopes for? But if we hope for that we see not, then do we with patience wait for it." (Romans 8:24-25)

Erroneously, hope is viewed as the wishful thinking for something good to happen in the future, however hope that concerns the future is not passive or wishful thinking. A close examination of our lives indicates that we live in anticipation and hopeful expectation that our efforts of labor in planting and sowing, studying and dedication, devotion and commitment will at some point yield an outcome we have determined. All those enterprises require active engagements for the yielding of that which is yet to be realized. It is comforting to know that our hope is established by divine providence of God.

It is built on the ordinances, precepts and the work of salvation that God has established. We gain confidence about the future because it is based on God's promises and revelation. It is what God has already determined that we hope and expect. It is firmly established and cannot be supplanted by any other, except our own unbelief and disobedience.

Having faith in what God has done makes living in this world less burdensome. Sometimes when we look around at the vacillating system of the world, the infidelity of human nature and our relationship to one another, it brings on an anguish of spirit. However, we are encouraged by the prophet in Lamentations 3:21-24, *"This I recall to my mind,*

15

therefore have I hope. It is of the LORD'S mercies that we are not consumed, because his compassions fail not. They are new every morning: great is thy faithfulness. The LORD is my portion, saith my soul; therefore will I hope in him." Our trust and hope must not be in other human beings or in material possessions or money, (Psalm 146: 3&5). Rather, our hope must be in God,

His Word and His mercy. Let us not be like the foolish builder who went and built on sand and when the storm blew there was a great fall. Anything outside of Jesus Christ and His Word is sand. There is a storm coming that will try what our hope is based on and will try every man's work (1 Co 3:13).

Let our prayers be about our hope in God and His Word, hope in His mercy and hope in His compassion. Anything else is not a solid foundation.

Pursue Godliness

"And to temperance patience; and to patience godliness."
2 Peter 1: 6.

Godliness is an inward attitude of utmost reverence and honor towards God that is demonstrated outwardly by our actions as we do the things that are pleasing to Him. Without godliness a Christian will not grow. Godliness is the framework upon which all other virtues are built. On the contrary, ungodliness will result in spiritual dwarfism and other non-progressive characteristics. Spiritual growth is guaranteed when we combine godliness with the virtues mentioned in 2 Peter 1.

Paul expanded on the concept of godliness when he said that we will obtain great gain/wealth when we combine godliness with contentment. (1 Timothy 6:6 KJV) To reverence God is to respect Him, deem Him awesome, all-mighty and all-powerful. Some might argue that one cannot revere/respect a God who cannot be seen or touched. However, we see Him through His works. "The heavens declare the glory of God; and the firmament sheweth his handywork". (Psalm 19:1 KJV) David was humbled and in awe at the works of His hands when he said in Psalm 8, *"When I consider thy heavens, the work of thy fingers, the moon and the stars, which thou hast ordained; What is man, that thou art mindful of him? and the son of man, that thou visitest him?"*

How do you acquire godliness? You know you are on track to acquiring godliness when you see God for who He truly is and as a result see yourselves as an unworthy subject. Isaiah had a vision of God and his response was profound:

17

"Then said I, Woe is me! for I am undone; because I am a man of unclean lips, and I dwell in the midst of a people of unclean lips: for mine eyes have seen the King, the LORD of hosts. (Isaiah 6:5 KJV)

There are many morally sound citizens in this world but is morality godliness? A godly person is moral but not vise-versa. Those who are godly will display characteristics that are parallel to Christ's. For example, the apostles were dubbed "Christians" due to the fact that their mannerism resembled Christ's. Additionally, having a "form of godliness" is not godliness. We should aim to be devout men, women and children of God and not settle for being just moral beings or having partial godliness. We want to be fervent, unwavering, steadfast, and committed.

May God help us during our time of prayer and consecration to diligently pursue godliness.

Stepping out in Faith

"Simon Peter, a servant and an apostle of Jesus Christ, to them that have obtained like precious faith with us through the righteousness of God and our Saviour Jesus Christ" 2 Peter 1:1 (KJV)

The apostle Peter wrote these encouraging words to the new believers who were having some serious doubts and whose faith was shaken. It seemed to these inexperienced believers that God was not keeping His promises and so they began to question whether they were true. Similarly, we all have times when we question one or another of God's great promises. Through trying circumstances, we wonder if God has abandoned us, or if His grace really is sufficient. Our fears and uncertainties can easily make us wonder whether God knows and cares.

Peter initiates this letter by assuring his audience that they possess the very same gift that he and the other apostles have "like precious faith." The faith of an apostle is not a different faith from that of recent converts to the gospel of Jesus Christ. We should not think that the faith God gives to those in highly public office is to be esteemed and honored more than the faith God gives to those whose ministries are more unassuming. God is not a respecter of persons (Acts 10:34).

Neither does the fact that we live in a completely different era require a different, more modern faith. The church needs the same faith today as it did at the time Peter was in spired to write.

This precious faith is obtained, not earned and we obtain it through the righteousness of our Savior Jesus Christ. We are worthy only because God graciously gives His righteousness to us. We are right in the sight of God because He credits His own righteousness to our account, and He imputes it to each of His people.

The consequence of this divine act of justification is that we now stand before God as righteous as Christ is. Correspondingly, as a gift from the unchangeable God, our faith is also secure. Those made right in God's sight by Christ's righteousness are given this precious faith. Its value is beyond calculation. It is much more precious than gold (I Pet. 1:7).

What a glorious consolation we have knowing that we have obtained the same faith that the apostles had. Such knowledge should cause us to rejoice and persevere. That is why the apostle endeavored to remind us of this great truth. May we always treasure the faith that we have, for in doing so we surely will not lose hope nor be shaken in our faith.

Confidence in the Word of God

"Knowing this first, that no prophecy of the scripture is of any private interpretation. For the prophecy came not in old time by the will of man: but holy men of God spake as they were moved by the Holy Ghost" 2 Peter 1:20 - 21

In our world today, the Bible is no longer revered as the inspired, trustworthy and infallible Word of God. In fact, some view it as being outdated, discriminatory in content and intolerant towards the ways people want to live their lives. But, no matter the beliefs of men or how many attempts have been made to discredit the Bible, surely it has withstood the test of time and we can have full confidence that it is the infallible Word of God.

The Bible or "Word of God" is the only reliable authority on earth when you need a guide for morality and a compass for godly living. This everlasting, trustworthy foundation of truth is our only real direction for our paths through the maze of life. It alone tells us how to be saved and to become reconciled with the Creator. In John 17:17, Jesus prayed for His disciples that God would sanctify them through His Word, which is the truth. This is the only truth that is known to Him.

Unlike the rest of the world, we know that the Bible is the inspired Word of God and as such, we are to anchor our faith and confidence in the fact that God's words are true and it is impossible for Him to lie. In Matt 24:35, Jesus declared that "Heaven and earth will pass away, but My words will never pass away."

Having confidence in God's Word means knowing that God "hangeth the earth upon nothing" (Job 26:7). Job wrote this passage long before the era of astronomy and space travel. The scientists of Isaiah's day did not know the topography of the earth, but Isaiah wrote, "It is he that sitteth upon the circle of the earth..." (Isaiah 40:22). The word for "circle" in this context refers to a sphere or a globe.

Having confidence in God's Word means knowing that the Bible is not a book of the month, year or century. But it is the Book of the Ages. In 1 Peter 1:25 we are told, "The Word of the Lord endureth forever. And this is the Word which by the gospel is preached unto you." History records that there has never been any other book that has received such opposition as the Bible. We have read of men who laughed at it, others who have scorned it, those who have burned it, ridicule and enacted laws to stop it from being read in schools. Nevertheless, the Bible has survived every test, and it is still the only accurate and trustworthy, God inspired Word that we have today.

Unity

"Behold, how good and how pleasant it is for brethren to dwell together in unity!" Psalm 133:1 (KJV)

A person backed in a corner by two or more attackers will have a difficult task at self-defense. But when he is joined by another who supports his desire to win the fight, the chances for his victory increases significantly. This truth applies to our spiritual journey. This journey is a walk of faith and it would be detrimental to attempt it alone.

Our common enemy loves to see us isolated and divided and he always seeks an opportunity to move in for the kill. He whispers his lies of defeat, crowds our minds with doubt and fear and reminds us of our past. We begin to feel insecure and vulnerable and soon we limp to a halt. But in unity there is strength! If my brother or sister sees me lagging behind, he or she can help me regain my strength with words of encouragement. Ecclesiastics 4: 9-12 reminds us, "Two are better than one... For if they fall, the one will lift up his fellow...And if one prevails against him, two shall withstand him; and a threefold cord is not quickly broken."

The church body benefits from consistent unity among its members. We foster an atmosphere of security when we genuinely love and care for each other. Acts 4:32 & 34 gives a beautiful account of sharing in the early church. No one was in need because everyone willingly shared their possessions. This happened because "the multitude of them that believed were of one heart and of one soul..." (verse 32).

Unity also attracts God's attention. Acts 2 recounts the experience of the 120 persons who waited for the Holy Ghost in the Upper Room.

According to verse 1, "They were ALL with one accord..." and in verse 4, "they were ALL filled with the Holy Ghost..." Note that ALL were filled, not some. The group was united in its goals and expectations and God responded to that.

The state of our horizontal relationships determines the quality of our vertical relationship with God. That is why the enemy vehemently opposes unity, but if we want to touch heaven we must push back against the evil force of division.

"But if we walk in the light, as he is in the light, we have fellowship one with another, and the blood of Jesus Christ his Son cleanseth us from all sin." (1 John 1:7)

Develop Temperance

"Add to your faith virtue and to virtue knowledge. And to knowledge temperance" 2 Peter 1: 5-6.

Self-discipline, self-control, self-denial and abstinence are terms used interchangeably with temperance. Further definition demonstrates moderation in action, thought, or feeling. Moderation is the key to all that you do. "Let your moderation be known unto all men. The Lord is at hand." (Philippians 4:5 KJV) Temperance cannot be achieved overnight. It takes discipline, hard work and patience to get to where you should be. The apostle Paul said, "I discipline my body like an athlete, training it to do what it should." (1 Corinthians 9:27 NLT) Olympic gold medalist, fastest man alive Usain Bolt's record-breaking speed and accomplishments were not achieved in a flash. It took focus, dedication, and hard work to reap those extraordinary rewards.

You may sometimes struggle with overindulgence and poor self-control. It might be a craving for food, shopping or sports. Regardless of what those struggles are, they must be tempered. Solomon, the wise man said;

"Do you like honey? Don't eat too much, or it will make you sick." (Proverbs 25:16 NLT) God's radical ultimatum is, "…If your hand, even your stronger hand, causes you to sin, cut it off and throw it away…" (Matthew 5:30 NLT) What would He require of those who struggle with an impulse to let the tongue slip? Spoken words cannot be retrieved. They can lift you up or tear you down. "There is one whose rash words are like sword thrusts, but the tongue of the wise brings healing". (Proverbs 12:18 KJV) The tongue can at times be out of control and must be tamed, yet no man can subdue it. Man has the ability to tame wild animals but lacks the power to control the tongue. "the tongue can no man tame; it is an unruly evil, full of deadly poison". (James 3:7-8 KJV)

There is hope. To gain absolute control and develop temperance in all things you must allow the Spirit of God to guide you. "let the Holy Spirit guide your lives. Then you won't be doing what your sinful nature craves." (Galatians 5:16 NLT) Being led by the Holy Spirit can help you to become disciplined and controlled and keep you on track to reaching your goal of developing temperance. You might be forced to take radical measures and get rid of that which causes offense or simply share your goal with an accountability coach who is willing to ensure that you stubbornly stay the course. Do whatever is necessary to help you progress towards your goal to develop temperance.

Be Steadfast and Resolute

"For if these things be in you and abound, they make you that ye shall neither be barren nor unfruitful in the knowledge of our Lord Jesus Christ." 2 Peter 1:8 (KJV)

Have you ever been determined to accomplish a task or goal no matter what? Think of a time that you made up your mind to do something, and no matter what occurred, you did it anyway.

Do you remember your thoughts as you prepared and executed that task? Can you remember the challenges you had along the way and how you overcame them?

Today as you read, your task is to think of a spiritual goal you want to achieve. As you do so, consider how meaningful it is to you and what you hope to get out of it. Next, determine if these goals align with the will of the Lord for your life.

If you are not sure of this, use the following Scriptures to help guide you: Proverbs 3:5-6 "Trust in the Lord with all thine heart and lean not unto thine own understanding, in all thy ways acknowledge him and he shall direct thy paths." Psalm 37:4 "Delight thyself also in the Lord; and he shall give you the desires of your heart."

An alignment of your goals with the will of the Lord is guaranteed to end successfully.

As you consider your goal, use the following steps to guide you:

1. Identify goal -write it down

2. Set a deadline - put a date on when you will complete your goal

3. List obstacles/challenges you think you will face

4. Identify strategies you can do to eliminate the obstacles

5. Identify groups or people you need to work with

6. List skills you need to reach your goal

7. Develop a plan of action

8. Look at the benefits

9. Execute do what you need to do to achieve your goal

As you encounter challenges and obstacles along the way, you may be discouraged and feel like giving up. You will need to remind yourself to "Be strong and do not give up knowing that your work will be rewarded." 2 Chronicles 15:7

Habakkuk 2:2-3 summarizes well the process of achieving our goals.

"Write the vision, and make it plain upon tables that he may run that readeth it. For the vision is yet for an appointed time, but at the end it shall speak, and not lie: though it tarry, wait for it; because it will surely come, it will not tarry."

Attain Virtue

"And beside this, giving all diligence, add to your faith virtue" 2 Peter 1:5

A wise builder considers a few things before construction begins. He first finds a trustworthy supplier with a history of providing high quality building materials that can withstand the test of time. Before you build or add virtue, consider the source from which you obtain the materials. The Word of God is your source! From it you can obtain all of the goods you will need to ensure resiliency of your structure. Stormy weather will arise and can shake the foundation on which you stand. However, (Ephesians 4:14 NLT) assures us that; "...we won't be tossed and blown about by every wind of new teaching..."

The very first component to add to the foundation is virtue. The word virtue comes from the Latin root vir, which means moral excellence. It is to display behavior that reflects high moral standards and is synonymous with words such as, righteousness, decency, morality, integrity, and honor. These are some of the qualities that we should look for in others, especially the people of God. You might find it easy to entrust to others your wealth, emotions, health or most importantly, your eternity if they possess virtue. No one would invest his valuables with someone of ill repute as described in 1 Corinthians 6:9-11. These attributes reflect who we were before we encountered Christ but we are washed, sanctified, justified in His name and by His Spirit.

Build wisely and carefully on the foundation on which you stand. 1 Corinthians 3:10; 12-15 (NLT) reads; *"I have laid the foundation like an expert builder. Now others are building on it. But whoever is building on this foundation must be very careful...anyone who builds on that foundation may use a variety of materials—gold, silver, jewels, wood, hay, or straw. But on the judgment day, fire will reveal what kind of work each builder has done. The fire will show if a person's work has any value. If the work survives, that builder will receive a reward. But if the work is burned up, the builder will suffer great loss"*

It is not a mystery why God wants you to add the element virtue to your structure. In fact, your body is the temple of God. As you stray from God your body becomes vile.

However, His grace can change your vile body to become like His glorious body Philippians 3:21 (KJV). Therefore, when confronted with a durability test this glorious body will withstand any disaster. The temple of God is built with integrity that cannot be compromised by fickle or changeable conditions.

Abundant Peace

"Grace and peace be multiplied unto you through the knowledge of God, and of Jesus our Lord." 2 Peter 1:2 (KJV)

In Philippians 4:7, the apostle Paul writes, *"And the peace of God, which passeth all understanding, shall keep your hearts and minds through Christ Jesus."*

The compound word translated peace is the Greek word huperecho, and it signifies a peace that exceeds and surpasses any other foundation of peace. The inference is that people may try to find peace in other places, but no other source of peace can be found to compete with the peace of God. The peace of God totally outdoes every other effort to produce peace.

Scripture teaches us that this peace even surpasses "all human understanding."

The word translated "understanding" or "mind" is the classical Greek word dianoia. This word refers to the ability to think and comprehend. It also portrays the mind as the source of all human emotions. The

Greek word categorically describes the mind as the seat of our intellect and emotions. Therefore, it is to be understood that the state of the mind determines the state of our lives.

What will this powerful peace produce in our lives? The apostle Paul says that this peace "shall keep your hearts and minds." (Philippians 4:7)

Paul uses this phrase to communicate clearly to us that God's peace will position itself at the gates of our hearts and minds, acting as a military guard to control and monitor everything that tries to enter our thoughts and emotions. When God's peace is reigning in us, nothing can enter into our hearts and minds without its approval!

This means we can refuse to succumb to the trials and tests which often cause panic and anxiety. When the peace of God is standing guard at the entrance of our hearts and minds, the enemy has lost access to our thought lives and emotions. The peace of God, protects, keeps, and defends us.

Nothing can compete with this powerful, guarding peace that God has given to us. When this peace operates in us, it dominates our inner thought life and consequently, our whole existence. His peace conquers our entire being, disabling the devil's ability to disturb us.

In every circumstance you may face, let God's abiding peace rise and dominate your heart, protect your mind; monitoring, guarding, and approving what does and does not gain access.

Divine Encounters

"And this voice which came from heaven we heard, when we were with him in the holy mount."2 Peter 1: 18 (KJV)

Have you ever been in a place and was assured that there was a devine presence or encounter? For example, you were distressed or cast down about a situation, and began to praise and worship or pray, when suddenly you felt an overwhelming presence of the Lord and the burden you felt lifted or remained the same.

However, you got up from your knees with courage and strength that you never had before. Or, you had a need and as you read the Scriptures, you found the answer in the Word of God, coupled with unexplainable peace. We can have divine encounters through the preached word, through a song, or even by a word of prophecy. Some of these encounters are obvious while others are not. Our lives can never be the same after these experiences.

Let us reflect on how Paul's life changed after having a divine encounter while travelling on the Damascus road. As we recall, he was the person who persecuted the church and was also responsible for Stephen's death.

Now, let us capture the essence of his response. "And he said, who art thou Lord? And the Lord said, I'm Jesus whom thou persecutest: it is hard for thee to kick against the pricks." (Acts 9:5 KJV). It is clear by Paul's response that not only did he have a divine encounter but also a divine revelation. Therefore, the trajectory of his life was forever changed in a selfless and positive way.

You and I can impact our families, workplace, friends and acquaintances, communities, and world. If we shine by lighting our candles, there is no limit to the divine encounters that will be established. Lives are still being positively changed by Paul's encounter.

Let us pause for a moment and reflect. What are we doing with the effects of our encounter?

Consider Your Calling

"Wherefore the rather, brethren, give diligence to make your calling and election sure: for if ye do these things, ye shall never fall." 2 Peter 1:10 (KJV)

For us to confirm our calling, we first must know what that calling is and what it entails. As you read today's devotional, ask yourself; what is my calling? Am I fulfilling the requirements of my calling?

God has called us out of darkness into His marvelous light. (1Thessalonians 1:4 KJV) To be in darkness means that you are unable to see where you are going. Such path, a path in which you cannot see your way, can often lead to an undesirable end. But, God has called you. He has called you into a marvelous light. In contrast to darkness, a path in which there is light enables us to see where we are going. In addition, we can see any obstacles that we may encounter. At times, with light we can also see our end goal; the finish line.

Now that we are in the light and we can see, where do we go? What do we do? How do we walk in this light? Romans 6:12- 13 admonishes us to "Let not sin therefore reign in your mortal body, that ye should obey it in the lusts thereof. Neither yield ye your members as instruments of unrighteousness unto sin, but yield yourselves unto God."

As God has created us in His own image, He has not only called us, but elected us. As with going through any election process, first we must possess the qualities and requirements to meet the demands of the job.

35

For there to be an election, there must first be a calling. We all have a basic calling upon our lives as the Scripture declares, "the whole duty of man is to fear God and keep his commandments." (Ecclesiastes 12:13)

When you walk in your calling God will elect you to fulfill His purpose. God believes in you so He has voted for you because He knows you posses the qualities to get the job done.

Sometimes you may feel you are not ready, capable or equipped to walk in your calling or complete the task at hand. However, an election is a two-way process therefore you must choose to fulfill your role. As you do so, "Trust in the Lord with all thine heart and lean not unto thine own understanding. In all thy ways acknowledge him and he shall direct thy paths" (Proverbs 3: 5-6 KJV).

God has called you, now He has elected you. What do you do with this mandate? I encourage you to confirm God's invitation and His choice of you. Once you do so, you will have your life on a firm footing. If your calling and election is sure, you shall never fall. (2 Peter 1:10 KJV)

Pursue Brotherly Kindness

"And to godliness brotherly kindness; and to brotherly kindness charity." 2 Peter 7 (KJV)

In 2 Peter Chapter 1, the apostle Peter encouraged the brethren to grow spiritually. God has provided everything we need to become like Him, but the responsibility is on us to yield ourselves to the process. Our calling as disciples includes selflessness and genuine love for one another. Loving each other is not optional but is a command as stated in John 13: 34-35 (NLT) "Love each other. Just as I have loved you... Your love for one another will prove to the world that you are my disciples." Our love for each other is one of our identifying marks as a Christian, so a constant display of selfishness and unresolved feuds will confuse onlookers and at the same time stymie our spiritual growth. One of the goals of spiritual growth is to impact those who are yet to experience God's love through the way we love. It is no wonder

God has a low opinion of the person who claims to love God who he cannot see, but hate his brother or sister who he can see. That person is called a liar. (1 John 4:20) Sometimes it is painful or does not make sense. Sometimes it feels unfair.

Our innate desire for self-preservation coupled with our cultural belief that "one bad turn deserves another" dictates that we should be kind to those who are kind to us and retaliate against those who hurt us. One cannot deny that an unkind word or deed, especially undeserved, can cause pain, but this cannot be remedied with carnal reasoning. In Ephesians 4:32 (NLT) the apostle Paul admonishes,

"Instead, be kind to each other, tenderhearted, forgiving one another, just as God through Christ has forgiven you."

We may be at different points in our journey of spiritual growth but let us not compare ourselves with each other. Instead, let us use the mirror of God's Word to show us our weak points as we strive to love each other as He loves us.

You Shall Stand, I Promise

Wherefore the rather, brethren, give diligence to make your calling and election sure: for if ye do these things, ye shall never fall. 2 Peter 1:10 (KJV)

After God has elected you and you are appointed to His office, the work begins!

Now you must make decisions you have never made before and act in ways that you have never before. Your speech and public display must be different. You now must develop goals and find ways to achieve them. The expectations from your elector are high.

As you begin to work in your elected capacity remember "with great power comes great responsibility."

Believe in yourself and your ability to complete your task at hand while keeping in thought that you are elected because you can do the job.

Along the way there will be obstacles and you will feel that what you are doing is useless or that there is no gain. When you begin to feel this way, do not give up, but rather continue to work, being confident that, "He who began a great work in you, called you and elected you will perform it until the end." (Philippians 1:6 NIV) He will not leave you nor forsake you.

Do not be cast down, rather, put your hope in God. "Be strong in the Lord and in the power of His might." (Ephesians 6:10 KJV)

"Be on your guard; stand firm in the faith, be courageous, be strong." (1 Corinthians 16:13 NIV)

"Do not be weary for in due season you shall reap if you faint not." (Galatians 6:9 NIV) "

Run that ye may obtain the prize." 1 Corinthians 9:24 (KJV), and as you do so, see the finish line. You have been given a mandate to be steadfast and unmovable, always abounding in the work of the Lord. (1 Corinthians 15:58 NIV) Stand your ground, work as hard as you can for Jesus while being confident that nothing you do for Him is a waste of time or effort. You shall stand because God has promised an expected end.

Abundant Grace

"Grace and peace be multiplied unto you through the knowledge of God, and of Jesus our Lord." 2 Peter 1:2
(KJV)

We are pardoned, redeemed, justified, and sanctified through the wonderful grace of God. His grace delivers to us peace with God because our sin, which caused enmity between God and us, has been removed through the sacrifice of Christ. Now our hearts are filled with peace, where once turmoil and confusion reigned. Our guilt has been replaced with assurance of forgiveness. Our desperate search for meaning and purpose has been satisfied in the person of Jesus Christ. Oh, the wondrous gift of His grace we experience because of our salvation.

Not only do we experience God's grace at the point of our initial salvation, but we continue to enjoy this benefit throughout our Christian journey.

The apostle Peter declares that grace and peace can be "multiplied". God's grace can therefore increase and abound in us and there is no way that we can exhaust God's supply of grace. We appreciate the revelation of His grace at the time of our conversion, but our need for grace does not end there. We still need His grace to be manifested to and in us as we are tested.

How can we have genuine assurance of God's abiding grace? Scripture teaches us that we obtain this through the "knowledge of God, and of Jesus our Lord" (II Peter. 1:2). We will experience moments when we do not sense God's presence with us, nor "feel" that He is near. We risk discouragement and despair if we do not stand on the assurance that God said in His Word, "I will never leave thee, nor forsake thee" (Hebrews 13:5).

The more we know of God and the more familiar we are with His promises, is the more our thinking is molded by the words of the Lord Jesus, and the more grace will be multiplied to us. The Scriptures contain the source of the grace we need. Jesus intends for His words to dwell in us, because they are the words of life. It is the truth that sets us free.

We have obtained from the Lord a faith of equal standing with the greatest apostles. And we have been given the very same promises. So, let us endeavor to keep "growing in the grace and knowledge of our Lord and Savior Jesus Christ" (2 Peter 3:18), and may grace be multiplied to you.

I am a Witness

"For we have not followed cunningly devised fables, when we made known unto you the power and coming of the Lord Jesus Christ, but were eye witnesses of his majesty" 2 Peter 1: 16 (KJV).

The disciples of Jesus were eyewitnesses to His majesty. One outstanding example of their direct witness of His divine glory occurred when He was transfigured before Peter, James and John on a high mountain. This glory caused His face to shine above the brightness of the sun with His clothes becoming as bright as light. Peter, in describing the event in 11 Peter 1:17 said that Jesus received from God the Father, divine honor and inexpressible glory when a voice from heaven declared, "This is my beloved son in whom I am well pleased." This glorious manifestation of God was similar to the unusual presence of God on Mount Horeb recorded in Exodus 3: 4-5.

Our experience as witnesses may not be similar to that of the disciples. Nevertheless, we are witnesses of His love, grace, mercy, goodness, kindness and compassion. "We were without Christ, aliens from the commonwealth of Israel, strangers from the covenant of promise, having no hope, and without God in the world. But...who sometimes were a far off are nigh by the blood of Christ" (Ephes. 2: 12-13 KJV).

Therefore, we have a right to individualize this phrase "I am a witness." We are called to be witnesses of His great love, care, and mercy. How can this be done? By extending ourselves to others – be it spiritual, emotional, physical, or economical. We can also testify to others about the love of

God; how He has saved us, pulled us from the horrible pit of sin, and how He can do the same for them. The need is urgent. "And others save with fear, pulling them out of the fire; hating even the garment spotted by the flesh." (Jude 1: 23 KJV).

The Glorious Hope of the Believer

"We have also a more sure word of prophecy; whereunto ye do well that ye take heed, as unto a light that shineth in a dark place, until the day dawn, and the day star arise in your hearts" 2 Peter 1:19

The glorious hope of every born again believer is the confidence that Jesus is coming again. The apostle Paul refers to it as the full assurance of hope (Heb. 6:11).

Usually, the word "hope" is used and accepted to mean that something might come to pass. Although the chance of winning in a raffle is remote, yet people play these games with the "hope" of winning.

However, the word "hope" as used in the New Testament means something that will positively and absolutely come to pass. Therefore, when the Bible refers to the return of Jesus Christ as our hope, it is saying that we can be assured that His return is absolutely certain.

In our world today, we witness nations rising against nations. We also have seen where the love of many has grown cold due to the increase in wickedness. In Matthew 24, the signs of the second coming of Christ include these happenings and many more. However, the believer in Christ can rejoice in these dark times, because the Bible tells us that when these things come to past, our redemption is nigh. (Luke 21:28)

Peter in describing the "day dawning" and "the day star arise in your hearts" alludes that it is the second coming of our Lord Jesus Christ. Further, when Jesus, who is the morning star, comes, He will give us light and we will have no more need of the prophetic Word. A love letter is treasured while the beloved is out of sight, but when the beloved is present, the message is put aside in exchange for physical contact.

Our hope is made sure when we allow Christ to be in the rightful place in our hearts and lives. Christ not only enriches our short-lived days on earth, but He gives us a glorious future far better than our earthly journey.

"If only for this life we have hope in Christ, we are of all people most to be pitied" (1 Cor. 15:19 NIV). But thank God, we can boast and glory in the promise of eternal life in heaven with Christ forever.

The big questions remain; do you take time to study the Word of God? Are you living in light of His coming, when we all will stand before Him to give an account of our lives? The Lord has given us some promises that are far better rewards than all that we can possess in this earthly life. He created us to worship Him in the most intimate way possible. It is our hope to live eternally with Him.

The Infallible Word Part

"Knowing this first that no prophecy of the scripture is of any private interpretation. For the prophecy came not in old time by the will of man: but holy men of God spake as they were moved by the Holy Ghost" 2 Peter 1:20-21

The word infallible signifies "incapable of making mistakes or being wrong." If something is faultless, it is never wrong and in this manner completely reliable. Similarly, the word inerrant as applied to Scriptures signifies "free from blunders." In other words, the Bible contains no errors. The Bible is the infallible

Word of God that was written by men, as God divinely inspired them. Additionally, we see faultlessness expounded in 2 Timothy 3:16–17, "All Scripture is God-breathed" and has the impact of creating servants of God who are "thoroughly prepared for each great work." God "breathe" Scriptures guarantee that the Bible is trustworthy, for God cannot breathe out errors.

The Bible is completely perfect and factual from cover to cover. Moreover, the Word of God is alive and active. Hebrews 4:12 declares that, "The Word of God is quick, powerful and sharper than any double-edged sword. It pierces even the soul and spirit, and it is a discerner of our thoughts and intents of our heart."

The Bible is the written Word by which God reveals Himself and His salvation plan for lost humanity. It is the word of salvation and will be accurate and useful forever. It is the only way by which we can cleanse ourselves from the filthiness of sin.

The Word of the Lord is perfect, converting the soul; it is sure, making wise the simple. The Word is right, rejoicing the heart and it is pure, enlightening the eyes. More to be desired than gold and sweeter than honey and the honeycomb is the Word of the Almighty God! (Psalm 19:7-10) Sadly, in today's society, there is an intentional effort aimed at discrediting the Word of God. Hollywood and publishing houses have circulated outrageously false materials attacking the credibility of the Bible. But rest assured there is coming a day when all infallible truth shall be revealed.

When the Almighty God, our Creator returns, it will be a glorious day for the believer, who by faith accepted Jesus Christ as their Lord and Savior!

Releasing control to God

"For the sinful nature is always hostile to God. It never did obey God's laws, and it never will. That's why those who are still under the control of their sinful nature can never please God." Romans 8:7-8 (NLT)

"Throw off your old sinful nature and your former way of life, which is corrupted by lust and deception. Instead, let the Spirit renew your thoughts and attitudes. Put on your new nature, created to be like God truly righteous and holy." Ephesians 4:22-24 (NLT)

We all have desires. Some desires are healthy and should be pursued. Others are deadly and should be avoided. A desire is a strong feeling that drives us to attain or possess something which is, or we think is, within our reach. Evil is the absence of good, that which is sinful, vicious, corrupt, morally wrong and wicked. So obviously, when you put together two words as powerful as evil and desire there is a reaction that is double powerful.

The Word of God recognizes the power of evil desire when it tells us in James 1:13-15, that, *"When tempted, no one should say, 'God is tempting me.' For God cannot be tempted by evil nor does He tempt anyone; but each one is tempted when, by his own evil desire, he is dragged away and enticed. Then, after desire has conceived, it gives birth to sin and sin, when it is full-grown, gives birth to death."* Therefore, we cannot be tempted without having evil desire already in place. The temptation will have no power without the evil desire. This is a very important point for all of us to remember as we fight temptation. We must deal with the evil desire.

Scripture tells us that our body needs to be offered to God as a living sacrifice.

This means that we make a conscious decision to no longer offer our body to sin as instruments of unrighteousness. Our mind needs to be renewed. As we are faithful and diligent to be made new in the attitude of our minds, we will begin to be transformed. We should no longer live according to the sinful nature, having our mind set on what nature desires but have our mind set on what the spirit desires.

There is so much life, energy and peace when we train our mind to live according to our new born-again spirit. When we successfully learn to do this, the born-again spirit acts as a sixth sense, tuning us in to God and enabling us to perceive reality from a divine perspective.

Grow with the Word

"Knowing this first, that no prophecy of the scripture is of any private interpretation. For the prophecy came not in old time by the will of man: but holy men of God spake as they were moved by the Holy Ghost" 2 Peter 1:20-21

The rule that must be acknowledged and recognized is that the Bible has come particularly to us from God and that each Word in it is completely perfect. Since God made us as intelligent creatures and He cherishes us enough to provide for us, undoubtedly He wishes to speak with us. He desires to have that personal relationship with us as He did with Adam and Eve in the Garden of Eden.

The many writers from different backgrounds composed the sixty-six (66) Books of the Bible in various terrains over a time of 1600-2000 years. These writers possibly never observed the compositions of the others, yet there is no inconsistency between any two. There is a persistent string, or message, all throughout the Bible that demonstrates there is one

Author and one message. That one message can be condensed as "For God so loved the world that he gave his only begotten Son, that whosoever believeth in him should not perish, but have everlasting life" (John 3:16).

Having this understanding, we must earnestly study the Scriptures to develop spiritually and come into an intimate relationship with Him. The Word of God is food for our soul, and we should hide it in our hearts, so that we might not sin against Him, as David in Psalms encourages us.

51

Study the Word of God using the literal method of interpretation – following the natural or usual implication of an expression, rather than seeking hidden or "spiritual" meaning. It is important that we use sound logic and study the words, grammar, background, context, history, geography, culture and parables.

Now that we believe no prophecy of the Scripture is of any private interpretation, we should study the Scripture with these thoughts in mind: pray for an illumination from the Spirit of God as you read His Words; understand that the Bible is meant to be understood; Scriptures interpret

Scriptures; no doctrine stands on one passage alone or is hidden in obscure passages, and there is one primary meaning for each Scripture, but there can be many applications.

We can have confidence that God has revealed, preserved and transmitted His Word to us today and that we can understand it. His Word is the Bible. His Word is infallible!

God is a Great Provider

"According as his divine power hath given unto us all things that pertain unto life and godliness, through the knowledge of him that hath called us to glory and virtue" 2 Peter 1: 3

There is a movement that has sought to minimize the role of fatherhood in our society, especially in a father's ability to provide for his family. Because of this cultural mindset we often struggle to embrace the idea of God's ability to provide.

However, this does not change the fact that God can and will continue to provide. Too often it is God who reminds us that He is the Provider. What is at work in our own consciousness is the inability to relate to a Father who provides. It dampers our capability to trust, thus making it difficult for us to yield to God.

In the beginning, it was not so. First, Abraham in a conversation with his son Isaac while on their journey to offer a sacrifice on to God stated,

"God himself will provide the lamb for the burnt offering, my son." (Genesis 22:8 NIV).

Then, Moses in rehearsing the historical events in the lives of the Children of Israel stated that *"The LORD your God has blessed you in all the work of your hands. He has watched over your journey through this vast wilderness. These forty years the LORD your God has been with you, and you have not lacked anything."* (Deuteronomy 2:7 NIV)

Conversely, as with the Children of Israel, God has done these actions in our lives. 2 Peter 1:3 confers by stating, "…his divine power hath given unto us all things that pertain unto life and godliness, through the knowledge of him, that hath called us to glory and virtue." Knowing that Jesus is my provider, I can now personalize the words of the psalmist by saying: I will not be forsaken. I will not be seen begging for bread because God is my provider. Furthermore, and in a relative context, my disposition does not change God's position. He is immutable, all-sufficient, the pre-existing one and Jehovah-Jireh (The Lord will provide).

Rosze Kaur

Made in the USA
Middletown, DE
05 November 2023

41803831R00036